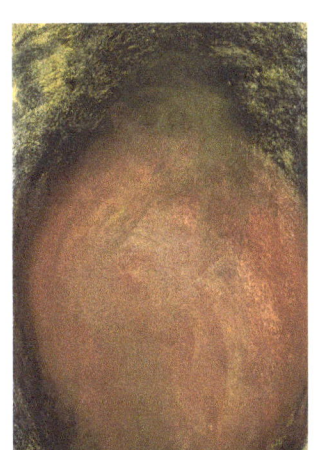

consciousness

martin nakell

SPUYTEN DUYVIL
New York City

© 2021 Martin Nakell
Images: t thilleman
ISBN 978-1-952419-62-1
Library of Congress Control Number: 2021942116

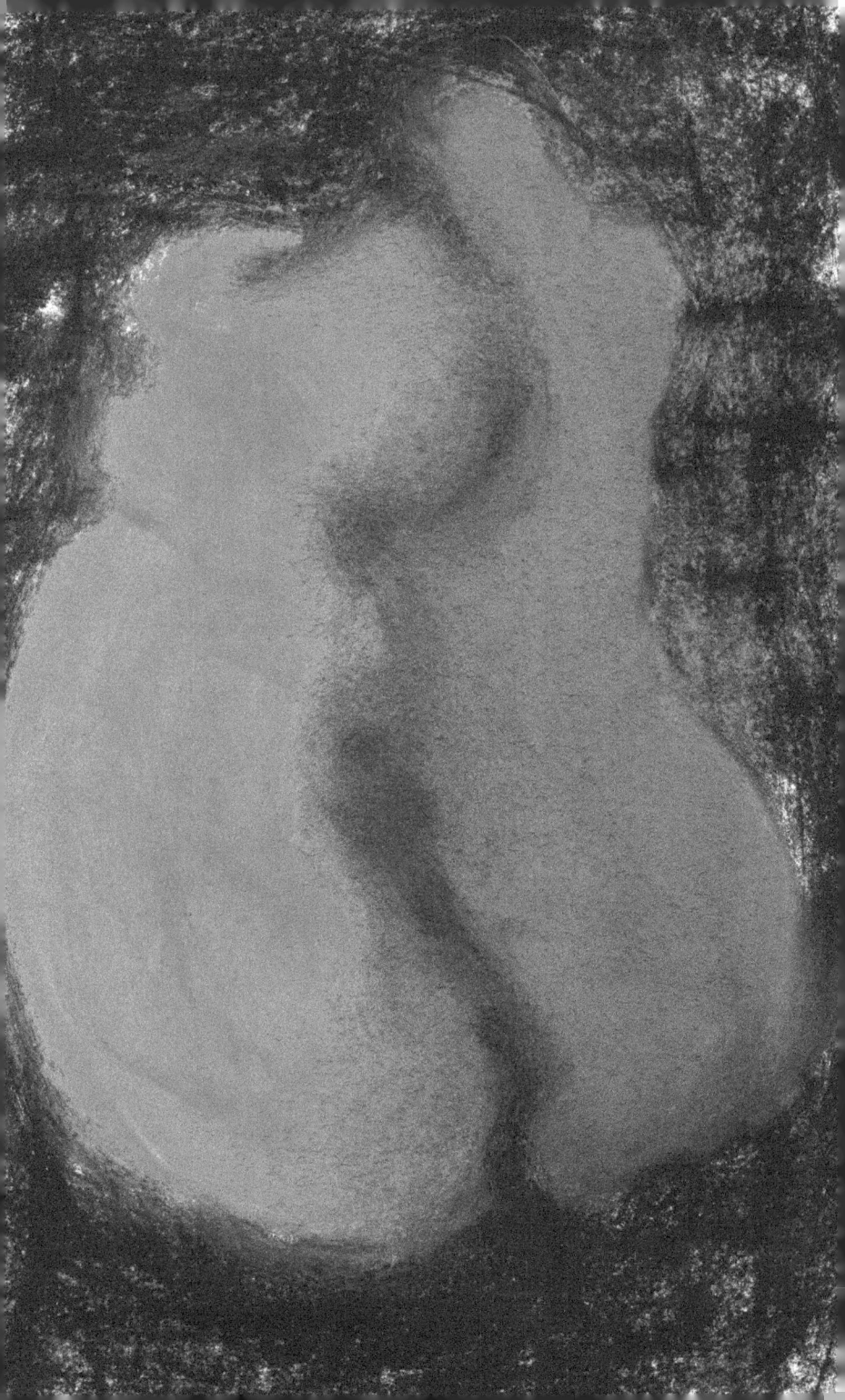

radiance emptiness the eye of the storm

the core of our being is radiance
the core of our thought is radiance
the core of our work is radiance
the core of our knowing is radiance
the core of our science is radiance
the core of our art is radiance
the core of our love is radiance
the core of our rage is radiance
the core of our hunger is radiance
the core of our darkness is radiance
the core of our morality is radiance
the core of our prophecy is radiance
the core of our weariness is radiance
the core of our futility is radiance
the core of our chaos is radiance
the core of our word is radiance
the core of our family is radiance
the core of our love is radiance
the core of our action is radiance

the core of our being is emptiness
the core of our thought is emptiness
the core of our work is emptiness
the core of our knowing is emptiness
the core of our science is emptiness
the core of our art is emptiness
the core of our love is emptiness
the core of our rage is emptiness
the core of our hunger is emptiness
the core of our darkness is emptiness
the core of our morality is emptiness
the core of our prophecy is emptiness
the core of our weariness is emptiness
the core of our futility is emptiness
the core of our chaos is emptiness
the core of our word is emptiness
the core of our family is emptiness
the core of our love is emptiness
the core of our action is emptiness

the core of our being is the eye of the storm
the core of our thought is the eye of the storm
the core of our work is the eye of the storm
the core of our knowing is the eye of the storm
the core of our science is the eye of the storm
the core of our art is the eye of the storm
the core of our love is the eye of the storm
the core of our rage is the eye of the storm
the core of our hunger is the eye of the storm
the core of our darkness is the eye of the storm
the core of our morality is the eye of the storm
the core of our prophecy is the eye of the storm
the core of our weariness is the eye of the storm
the core of our futility is the eye of the storm
the core of our chaos is the eye of the storm
the core of our word is the eye of the storm
the core of our family is the eye of the storm
the core of our love is the eye of the storm
the core of our action is the eye of the storm

the core of our cosmos is radiance
core of our eye is the storm of emptiness
the emptiness of our eye the core of the storm
the storm of our core is the core of emptiness
the emptiness core storm radiance

the core of our cosmos is emptiness
the core of our radiance is the eye of our storm
the emptiness of our storm is the eye of the core
the eye of the core is emptiness
the storm radiance eye eye

the core of our cosmos is the eye of the storm
the emptiness of our storm is the eye of radiance
the core of our eye is the storm of emptiness
the radiance eye core eye
core radiance emptiness eye storm storm eyed

blackness

Something black radiates with blackness. something black without a tincture of white in it some blackness that was once a whiteness without a tincture of blackness in it.

And I didn't say not-black. sometimes I imagine I didn't say anything but stood there with myself in all the blackness of blackness in motion. When my father, on his deathbed, said forgive me all my wrongs against you. Then I did say black. And I said, blackness.

In Jewish folklore there are two types of golem. There is the black golem and there is the black golem. Throughout history they have known times of unsurpassable joy they have shared between them in a freedom we know glimpses of in every act of our bodies. They can turn horrifyingly dark murderous vengeful absolutely demonic. The way to meet this terror is with an open heart. It may take centuries. Once we have admitted them welcomed them in to our bodyminds it may take generations for a whole culture to see they mirror each other, they reflect each other's blackness of joy or blackness of terror until they see it is a blackness irrefutable, a blackness palpable, a blackness of brick and leaf.

Watch the blackness for a long time. The longer you watch the more you will see emerge from blackness the more it will surprise you. There is a chair there on the hill in the city. Sit. They'll bring you a drink. Something to eat. Look out from the hill. At the blackness. Let the black nourishment penetrate into your cells. Start growing an awareness of the blackness. Let it astonish you.

One word follows another pours forth each one carries with it a mouthful of blackness each one sent forth on a mission searching for blackness each word that word, noble, which had discovered blackness.

There is a blackness that lies still and quiet. There is a blackness that is neither black nor white. It's the blackness we talk about when we say black and the blackness we talk about when we say not-black. It's a blackness that lies still and quietly throughout space and time which means not the black of the past nor the black of the present nor the black of the future.

Cause and effect are the same. Blackness is the cause of blackness is the effect.

Time is a time of blackness. Space is a space of blackness. Time/space is a time/space of blackness. That this newborn babyinfant in my care is dying is a sorrow of blackness I cannot fathom but am given to know. Where is the end of your generosity in the finite endlessness of blacknesses. When had it begun.

Does this mean that life and death are the same? It means that life is a blackness and that death is a blackness. What is the purity or the plenitude of that blackness

There are no doors into blackness. There are no doors out of blackness. Blackness has no past. Blackness has no future. Blackness absorbs all colors. Blackness absorbs all light. Blackness knows no time. Blackness has no space. Blackness was not born anywhere. There is nowhere blackness will die. I cannot say that I know this blackness. You cannot say that you are not this blackness. Blackness absorbs all language. All not-silence is absorbed in blackness.

Blackness and not-blackness are one.

It was always here, this blackness. As a dense cube. When it liquifies, I drink. My cells, dessicate, now hydrated with blackness, grow.

How old is blackness? How old is blackness? It's amazing! How old is blackness? I was born by a great lake from my mother's womb. Yesterday, she swam.

When I speak, I speak a language known as blackness. It has a clarity of sound you can almost hear. Almost is a word blackness invented. I can't tell you what it means. I can't tell you what anything means. You don't almost mean something. You mean something. When you try to explain to me what you mean, you speak blackness.

Because before you were born before your mother was born you were all blackness.

In blackness there is no joy. Only impure being contains joy. What might something like blackness know about impure or pure being? Everything blackness. What keeps blackness from pure being? From joy? Just the forest. Just the sea.

I close my eyes. That darkness isn't the blackness. With the creation of the universe as it expands along the synapses of our brain – that's very close to being blackness.

Something that is not blackness shares space/time with blackness. Molecule for molecule atom for atom it defies the exclusion principle of the basic laws of physics but I know it and you know it and here it is.

Last night. I went into the blackness. I was in my mind I was part of my mind. I said to myself so this is what it feels like. I went to the nursery. I spoke to myself who lay in his crib, sleeping. How can I remember what I said? All day I imagine one thing or another. I know I didn't say blackness. or I did, I took the risk. I said blackness.

the psychic structure of blackness is that it is colorless.

Not-blackness pours into the body of blackness. Fills it to overflowing and fills and fills it. And fills it. The not-blackness formed in the not-void with the not-blackness body of actual time flows into the body of blackness. Flows into me I close my eyes now not in a darkness but to the rushing sound of not-blackness the not-void and actual time beat through my breath I hear it all in the blackness that is the breath and the mind of this poem. That is her body as well. It is the meaning of words.

A breeze blows blackness across time

Unfold blackness. Render it everywhere. Lay it on horizontal surfaces. Lay it over a glass tabletop. Over a seasurface. Over a desert floor.

Over the face of the deep. Over the noise of the everyday. Over all. Fold blackness. Layer by layer by layer. Fold it.

ghostfeast

i took
a ghost
to the feast
laid out
in the 1st hell
of not-knowing.

i fed him
on rages
i fed him
on fullnesses
on emptiness.
the son/of-a-bitch
was a ravenous bastard
who'd seen through
the tricks
so i killed
him. had to.
the words wouldn't suffice
otherwise.
neither
would a very
        long
   silence

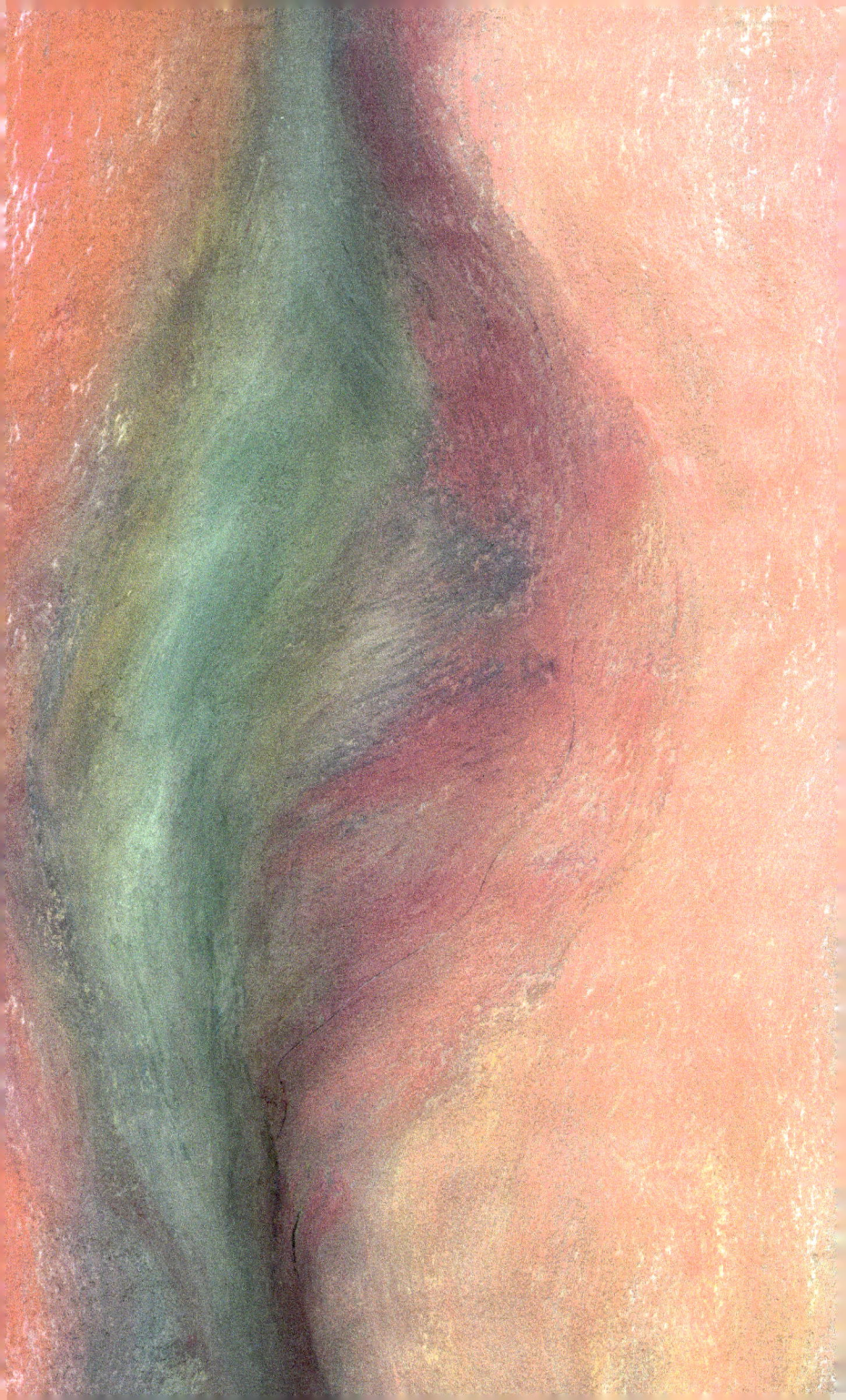

1132

1.

For 103 years the clock above the barbershop reads 11:32. Every day I see you I love you no more no less than yesterday. This is not a sensation of loss or gain. To write is not a sacrilege or a transgression as it once seemed to become. No one is. When you said, it's getting late, it's 11:32, you better go, and he said where, and you said, 11:32 and he said, no, that's your meeting, not mine.

When I entered the story it astonished me. For a moment the cat and I thought we lived in the same world but we do not because the cat has a different sense of time. And I came into the story looking for you standing in the absence of you, in an absence of time, waiting. Waiting for time? So I began to tell myself the story in which you never appeared. Narrator and main character. It was strange as out that window there was a clock above a barbershop and it read 11:32. If it doesn't move, there will be no narrative. Narrator, yes. And you, absent, can you be a character in this? When? Is there a character absent in every fiction? Not time. Someone else. Nor memory nor expectation. someone else. On each page of it. In each word of it.

Does every fiction begin at 11:32 end at 11:32?

The lawn is lush. You lie there arms splayed, nearly naked, beautiful to see. I imagine ravaging your body. The sun beats me to it. The sun has swallowed you and you are dissolved you are disappeared into its heat. I, there, waiting for an object of my lust. I find it.

2.

If you're not careful, he'll take everything you've got, even your eyes. Why? Has he nothing? Has he no eyes of his own? In what darkness did he forfeit them to a light he could not see, refused to know? There are things he would have to see he could not tolerate. Things you had long ago forgiven in a broad sweep of the whole at 11:32. In order. To. Can he steal the light in your eyes as well? And, if not, why steal your eyes? Just to better see a darkness? Perhaps. Sit with him for a while. Neither of you speaking. Until he sees the futility of his sight, stolen. Until you see. When he asks you, if your life has meaning, what is it? Just keep looking. Lest he steal it. Lest he see it is no longer him, no longer yourself as he hoped you would not be forever. and you are not. are you?

BECAUSE OF TRISTAN TZARA

give the mind room to move   seep out the pours of
the skull   let it float in the air   among the
abundance of parti-colored molecules
let it freshen in the zones of the garden
let it shock the wings of the irregular zoëfly
let it too breathe in the breathing night air
let it find turbulence on the horizon
then ride it to the end
of its end as its resurrection
let it expand through realms of chaotic chaos
let it discover the dew
that sips on hallucinations
of green
let it relax
under the shade
of the oliveladen olive tree
let it dream
once and for all
but an unfinished dream
that perpetuates the piazza empty
and the colonnade
let it wander let it expand so far
it will never return
to the insult of the mere brain
i have gained all the spiritual wisdom i need
i have read enough books to last me yet another three or five
lifetimes
i have told enough lies to condemn me to hell in a shrimp
boat

i am the mother and the father of all the others i will ever know
you are the mother and the father of the only other i will ever know
i am the one who saved the infant from drowning in the bulrushes
i sit with him on the banks of the river
in the hard hard rain
waiting for the future to declare a truce
i declare that poetry – and the whole history of poetry – will come to an end at the end of this line
i am the one who created eternity it was a joke i was playing on some gods who came to irk me
i am the one who kissed you in the dark so many years ago inside the approach of your puberty
i am the one who wrote the hebrew bible i take back every word of it none of it happened
except the creation i wrote that then i got carried away
i am the one who threw Caution to the wind but then Caution threw me to the Ends of the Earth
i am the one who sold his genius for a shekel or two zuzim but then stole it back from the fool who'd paid
so much for it
i am the superconductor who proved einstein wrong by proving einstein right i am the one who
invented the zero and the passive verb the fiction of the verb to be i am not the primum mobilum
what? do you think i would have that much pride that much hubris? but i did teach the primum
mobilum to count to one and to multiply and fill the void
and i consider myself a very likeable person

ON TEACHING

At the same / time / as the writer /writes the written, /the written /writes/ the writer /On rare occasion / a miracle will occur whereby / before the writer writes /the written, the written / writes the writer.

    Reuven ben Eif'echad
    at the Academy of Beatitude (Akahdauhmiyah B'racha)
    Jerusalem 222 – 152 BCE

ON IDENTITY

I am the one who teaches you who are the me that teaches wherein the learning survives

ON EROS

The transmission of question is carried on waves of eros this is the only way it can pass through the barrier it must encounter to be of significance

ON AGE

While the teacher comes with experience and the student comes with innocence they discover all the advantages and all the disadvantages of each, all of the desires of each for the other. Within the permissions of creation, they agree to abide by the dictates of time

ON FULFILLMENT

the fulfillment of teaching as the fulfillment of learning can be achieved only by returning to the originlessness of its beatitude in a communion of silence that is to say in a fullness of the one sense of sight that learning lead to insight which is a-textual outside even the margins of the text fulfilled only by the silence of the eye that absorbs the letter and the word and the world as it itself remains alive within its context which is consciousness

ON THE SUBJECT

when the teacher learns that what they have to teach is themselves, they are aware of the absence of limitations. they lay their hopes on their student that the student will come to know more than the teacher so as to fulfill the teacher. this is a delusion. insofar as everyone's knowledge belongs to them alone, no one can know more or less than anyone else. the teacher then knows they are teaching delusion. it's time to let the student go, to let new students come in

ON TRANSITIONS

The teacher realizes that the you of the student is the I of the teacher that the knowledge sought returns from the student to the teacher where the teacher cannot avoid seeing his own now redoubled resistance to knowledge that he sees it as an Other that would embrace him

ON HOWLS OF IGNORANCE

The teacher teaches that the howl of ignorance is a temptation not to be resisted but to be exhausted that while it feels to be the authenticity of knowledge it is nothing compared to the absence of knowing it already contains even in the highest register of its boldest scream

ON THE LOVER

The teacher believes that the knowledge he has acquired is his secret lover. She/he protects the domain of this union. When the student arrives, the teacher may be defensive, become angry, even guilty at being discovered in his illicit affair. The teacher and the student may together enter into a transgressive dance with knowledge. How far this goes – into destruction – into the fertile – depends on the teacher and the student, on their need for the lover. On their use of the lover. On their need for redemption. On their need for liberation. The destruction could be total and it could be self-inflicted. The excess of destruction could lead them into delight

ON TRADITION

Learning is not preserving, but making new. Therefore, it is an act of destruction. To study law, we destroy the law. To study history, we destroy history. To study consciousness is to destroy consciousness. That is to say, learning is like desire. It's a fire that burns itself until there is nothing left to burn. This moment is the crisis of creation

WHERE TO COME FROM

To teach is to come from where the student is, not from where the teacher is. How can the teacher know where the student is? (1) By knowing where the teacher is. (2) By entering into a pact with the temptation of ignorance – that you allow it to be permanently forgiven

ON THE EMPTINESS OF THE TEACHER
To teach, the teacher empties himself of knowledge. Only then should the student trust the teacher. But the teacher – emptying himself of all knowledge, stands thus, the wind blowing through him

ON THE TEACHER'S SECRETS
To teach, the teacher must reveal himself to the student. This means to reveal to the student all the secrets about himself that he hides from everyone, even if from himself

ON FAITH IN TRUTH
To teach the truth of any given thing – that not fire, nor water, nor aether, but energy, for example, is the primary element of being, the teacher must believe that it's not true, then discover it as he first encountered it, as a truth he was unable to grasp, around which he could not wrap his mind, as a truth impossible to know, needing to be tested with one's senses one's perceptions one's questioning mind every second, until it becomes the teacher's/the student's mind

ON THE ARROGANCE OF KNOWLEDGE
The teacher must convey the arrogance of knowledge, then let the student discover the terrifying unbearable suffocation of the arrogance of knowledge – the only escape from that arrogance being to encounter – on the student's own in their own time – that moment of awareness of the uselessness of knowledge

ON THE QUESTION OF (THE) GOD(S)

Once, I asked one of my students what was the difference between the Greek and the Hebrew Gods. He discoursed for a good long time, talking about how the Greek Gods were more concrete, the Hebrew God more abstract; the Greek gods are about power; the Hebrew god is about justice and foreignness; the Greek Gods are about the themselves-as-universal; the Hebrew God is about the universal-as-the-universal; the Greek Gods are about Fate; the Hebrew God is about the tradition and the new; the Greek Gods are about the-present-in-the-eternal; the Hebrew God is about the eternal-in-the-present; the Greek Gods are about sensuous life; the Hebrew God is about the order of the sensuous life; the Greek Gods are about the forms for and the consequences of the overflow of powerful emotion; the Hebrew God is about the transformation of the overflow of powerful emotion into a celebration of the seasons; the Greek Gods are about life becoming a book; the Hebrew God is about the book as life. The Greek Gods have a cornucopia of qualities – thunder, the sea, fire, speed, sensual love; to the Hebrew God we can attribute no qualities; the Greek Gods are about sex; the Hebrew God says: be fruitful and multiply; I (my student says) cannot prove the existence of the Greek Gods or the Hebrew God; I cannot disprove the existence of the Greek Gods or the Hebrew God

Following my student's discourse, we were hungry, and we ate. After a good lunch with good wine, I asked my student which – to her – was real, the Greek Gods or the Hebrew God. She stared at me. She was trapped. You could see her poor mind run back and forth. She expected that I had the answer, that I just waited for her response, which I would either accept as correct or reject as wrong. We stood for some time like that. Perhaps we're still standing like that. Perhaps that's my student's answer to me. If so, she passes through the gate

ON BELIEF

When there is nothing left between the teacher and the student – when the thirst for knowledge becomes – even momentarily – absent as the desire for transmission becomes – even if momentarily – absent – the beast of learning appears, ferocious, unappeasable, unassailable, authentic, without abstraction but wholly real. When the beast dissolves – for now – it leaves immeasurable traces of unimmeasurable belief

ON SOLITUDE

When the student sees that it is time for them to leave their teacher, the teacher will stand in the doorway to their Academy in solitude. The student turns to see the teacher in the doorway, alone. If the student has a flash of an illumination that this solitude is what he has given to his teacher as tuition, the teacher will see the student illuminate, even in daylight. The teacher will find himself well-paid

ON THANATOS

When language breaks open its bonds of grammar and logic wait for the student to relay what they see in the absence of oppositions

ON NOSTOS

When the student, having washed off the barnacles of his sea-journey, enters his old Academy of Beatitudes, the new teacher doesn't recognize him at all. This new teacher asks if the student-returned is seeking a teacher, for his son perhaps, his daughter? The student-returned tells the new teacher that he is here looking for a teacher for himself, claiming that he never sufficiently learned what he had studied here years ago. The new teacher of the Academy asks him if he'd rather not have a job as a teacher in the Academy. The student-returned takes a broom from the corner with which he sweeps the floor. He leaves the Academy for the second and perhaps for the last time

1897
a poem in four voices

ohtoh: last night i dreamt that israel's neighbors were at peace with israel, and even moreso, that israel was at peace with herself

ohtah: amazing what these words can do how they ride the light

ohtoh: so different than the israel we've yet to know

ohtah: words aren't symbols of anything yet look at all the rambunctious stuff that they do that they get themselves into

IRAN DOMINATES OBAMA-NETANYAHU MEETING

ohtoh: all israelis would be different because of this peace i dreamt of

ohtah: and yet where do they come from all these words we know i'd love to just once to see where they come from that wordless origin wouldn't that be something

ohtoh: because as he'd said we haven't been afraid to make war and we are not afraid to make peace

2011 BRINGS PROMISE TO STOCKS WITH HIGH-DIVIDEND YIELDS

ohtah: like the words is & is not don't all words contain their opposites because of where they come from

ohtoh: my father told me – we were sitting in jerusalem – at a café – that my father's persian friend – from tehran – signed all his letters to my father with the farsi salutation: *infinite bliss*. do you think such a thing exists? my father asked me. a bliss that is infinite? and can it co-exist with the stream of the extraordinary/ordinary of things within that stream? or are those just meaningless words – infinite bliss? if the temple were rebuilt from the western wall would there be a reign of infinite bliss? and yet isn't bliss infinite so long as it lasts? is the universe – as one of the rabbis of the first temple once said – always in a state of infinite bliss? and aren't we – as the same rabbi said – the supplications of that bliss?

ohtah: and then just think about how a language forms the way we think, for example, if i say the word father what do *i* see and what do *you* see? all from just one little 6 letter word.

ohtoh: and why did i have that dream i had to ask myself. i had it because i so want that peace i want it so and i didn't even know how much i wanted it until i dreamt my want my desire my outrageous demand my childish tantrum

PRIME MINISTER: ISRAEL HAS ACTED AGAINST U.S. ADVICE BEFORE

ohtah: have you ever seen a word arrive and be and then depart i mean literally well i mean literally in your mind seen a word arrive in a somewhat unformed unshaped way and then become the word and then depart again into dissolution. have you ever? no? have you never? they arrive like annunciations but of what what of?

ohtoh: and i don't just mean a cold peace i mean where all the arab states felt warmly toward israel and israel felt warmly toward all the arab states and what wouldn't all that be like, huh? well i'm not crazy i'm just saying it was my dream. i'm not naïve. i'm not outside the pale of passions outside the aether of rages.

ohtah: did you know that carl jung told james joyce: james, he said, jimmy boy, he said, your schizophrenic daughter lucia she is drowning in the seas that you jimmy jim joyce that you swim in meaning of course the seas of language freed from what? freed from language's normative role of meaning only one thing in only one way at only one time

ohtoh: once, i was walking in haifa with two friends: one israeli and one palestinian. i said to them both: think of the word israeli what comes to mind and then think of the word palestinian what comes to mind and you know what they both said about both words: an enigma they said. about both those words. and that's what they were calling *themselves*

TAX CHANGES FOR NEW IMMIGRANTS

ohtah: look. the moon now is rising. i mean the sun now is rising. look. there. do we call that the sun or the moon? rising

ohtoh: in a turkish café in jerusalem he said to me: whoever owns jerusalem owns the world & i said i own jerusalem it's a city full of ancient languages of quarried beliefs & their disbeliefs of predestined harmonies even of flying carpets for sale of maggots feeding on stone & marble of shades resisting people of poetries elevating fig trees to the level of foremothers of tourists looking for modern jewish prostitutes who might whisper magical signs

ohtah: there are the languages of magical signage to be found in the medieval gardens of italy & spain but their symbols are so far indiscernible although i know what they say would you like to know what they say? no? ok. of course not

ohtoh: i'm going to repeat it: israel at peace not only with her neighbors but with herself. golden hospitals. a nobel prize in every home. A cool wind along the axis of fervencies. an israel that exists and does not exist that revels in the plethora of its existence & its non-existence

INTERNATIONAL ATOMIC ENERGY AGENCY CHIEF: IRAN NOT TELLING ABOUT NUCLEAR PROGRAM

ohtah: is there a difference between the words existence & non-existence? what does kabbala say? what does st. augstine say? what does the poet say the one who couldn't be stopped from digging with his shovel in the vineyards looking for potsherds of his family's mythos

ohtoh: i mean also her neighbors at peace with israel and at peace with themselves *ohtah*: the languages are all inexhaustible even were someone to try to exhaust them

ohtoh: only the country – israel – herself is real: jerusalem, tel aviv, haifa, jaffa, the hills of judea, the white white moonscape along the road to the dead sea, the kids in the streets of acre, the garbage truck, the #7 bus, the finest falafel of homegrown labor and adolescent daydreams at the stand on the hilltop right where the jewish the armenian the christian and the muslim quarters converge to the sound of the music of the fishes

A RAPIST REDUCED TO BLAMING THE COURTS

ohtah: *if* we agree that language can't arrive at what was once called truth & that what language *can do* is describe the world word by word then what does it mean if i say: the lord is my shepherd or the woman is not a woman but an image come naked from the garden of shamelessness to imitate our world or the sun stood still or the ship gallops over the rooftops of that neighborhood night after skyseed or if i say they listen to the music from whence they had once gone inside the radio sound wave

ohtoh: perhaps despite appearances every man woman & child in the state of israel is at their core driven by a precise logic which one scholar said was the first gift given by yahweh to moses on sinai. that scholar climbed sinai. her mind clarified with a precise impulsive logic that includes the proposition: israel exists and it does not exist.

ohtah: the basis of language is logic; the basis of logic is grammar: the logic of grammar is beauty; the grammar of beauty is the midnight's intuition of existence.

ohtoh: the two pilgrims – one arab the other a jew – approach the temple mount and the kotel – the western wall, respectively, with a special kind of indifference found only in the sublime. two security police approach each pilgrim, accept their papers as valid, then grant each leave to proceed. These two will never meet. If they did, how would they describe how would they discuss how would they express their respective experiences to each other? think about it. if the time came when their forking paths crossed and the circumstances were necessary they would kill each other

ISRAEL CALLS ON UNITED NATIONS TO CONDEMN ROCKET ATTACKS FROM GAZA

ohtah: the israeli philosopher ben rueven writes: "at a certain moment in childhood, everyone looks into a mirror and sees for the first time themself as a separate being; they hear that voice that speaks to them as themselves." doesn't a nation a people also have such a moment? but what if, at a certain point in time much later, that nation sees that the voice of itself which speaks to itself falls away grows faint grows quiet. what is left? is it something altogether new which had always been there? ben rueven goes on to say that this could have been a question for kabbala. after all, it's a question of language in which the letters fall away. after that ben rueven wrote no more philosophy but enjoyed – every bit as he had enjoyed philosophy – a second career as a botanist specializing in the breeding of and revolutionary methods of cultivation of roses and especially of succulent white roses that would grow in the desert where he'd settled

ohtoh: the breeze blew through the garden of roses bearing scents from africa

ohtah: i called you by every conceivable name ad infinitum but you never answered. i began from the beginning i continue without bitterness

ohtoh: the grammar of wheat incites the scream of experience

JUSTIN BEIBER AND ISRAEL'S MISSED OPPORTUNITY

ohtah: my notebook was new, the pages were empty. i could have picked up a book to read. instead i went out for a walk looking for words. i found thousands of them. & hundreds & hundreds & hundreds of eons of millions of them

ohtoh: i suddenly was hungry for sights to fill my eyes. i walked out among all the buildings. i walked through the streets. i walked all the way to the beach then all the way back home. it was exhilarating. all that time i was no one i was all of no one. by the time i got back, i was weeping the tears of no one

ohtah: if you wait long enough the right word will come to you. this could take minutes hours days or years. you might not know the right word for what you want until a long time after you begin searching. but it will come. even if you have to make it up it will come. every word has an urge a fate to come

ohtoh: when i realized that i had a competition going with all my male friends i wondered if that weren't a kind of madness. not that i didn't love some of them all of them. but i had to ask myself what was this competition? what was i competing for? when the best thing i could get was friendship. i went around to all my male friends with a different thought in mind and damn it it worked. the competitiveness fell away. i lost nothing. i was more attached to everything even my country which for god's sake i'd fought for even having watched some of my friends with whom i'd been competitive fall in battle

IDF: WE ARE READY FOR POSSIBLE MILITARY OPERATION IN GAZA

ohtah: when we say friendship what do we mean. when we say love what do we mean. when we say self what do we mean. when we say enemy what does it mean. all these words mean something important

ohtoh: and then i got to thinking about my country. looking around me, everyone i saw was a countryman/woman. i thought of them as fellow countrymen. man woman and child. even dogs! that's the way thought is. that's an israeli dog. isn't that crazy. even people i mean israeli strangers whom i might see on the street and have no personal affinity even vast differences with i think of as countrymen/women. israeli arabs – they're countrymen. druze – they're countrymen. the ultra-orthodox – they're countrymen/women. a thief, a prostitute, a lawyer, a musician. yet what is it i share with these people that i don't share with others of a different even another country who are also different from myself? from the most ancient of times all this means something. you can't escape it. even if you go somewhere to find out who you are outside your country you come from somewhere as alien to your culture as you might get somewhere like india, say. it wouldn't change that one bizarre thing. it can't

ohtah: in the tensionspace being is nothingness act on the first miracle of a god-given language to a bookbody people

ohtoh: we are a stoneborne bookbound bookenamored booklost mesmerized people of the sacred parchment whose fires ignite our synapses we who are the contemporary kind of freethinkers liberated from the book in quest of the transluscent book

ohtah: the grammatology of sex walk the desert granulated earth to cools underfoot step calculates in terms negotiated under the sign of the broken egg under the aegis of a breathless tribe inventing geometric proportions between then and now between the here and the there the geometries of the brain to the responsibility owed to the heritage of poets

A TWO-LEGGED GREAT DANE

ohtah: someone once said that without language we live in a world only of a continuous continuum one thing melding without meaning into another. it's only language that gives us any chance at order at functioning at doing at being. but i don't quite believe that. something prior something more instinctual gives us all of that; *then* language comes to name it. language lets us communicate it. language allows us to say:

"i'll meet you at the park at noon." but i have carved out the meaning of a park and i know the sun before we had named it sun. where in the mind does all that take place. or, in the whole body.

ohtoh: and then i think well the legends abraham sarah isaac rebekah jacob leah they're all countrymen/women whom i never knew but they mean something so much different than what george washington means to me. king david. solomon. even if as I may have little idea of who king david or king solomon really were. what muhammad means to a muslim. odysseus to a greek. and i build myself on that. i can't help it. jesus christ is an interesting case. he was born in my country he died in my country but to me he's not a countryman. that's what they've done to him. that's how strange strangeness is, otherness is.

ohtah: it's nighttime. it's just turned night. elephants lumber across the sky. the night signals to the cartographers. the false gods turn over their names to the Dispenser of Names. lives there a true god who keeps the name? such a ridiculous question i won't even grace it with an answer

ohtoh: take passover, for example. archeologists here have concluded that the exodus from egypt never happened. they have a whole nother story about than this myth of the jews coming from egypt. no thousands upon thousands ever came. and every year we sit around a table and we eat certain foods and we say certain ritual sayings and we interpret the stories and we talk about freedom from all kinds of slavery and it all none of it ever happened. and i love that. i love it. it fills a void and leaves the void a void. and it is all about spring and we cannot talk about spring as a void spring happens. spring is. spring belongs to no one. no one makes it happen. there is no moses of spring. spring is an unalterable fact of being like being born human is unalterable. so i think of passover as a ritual of being human. no one else does but then every jew invents their own judaism. even if you have to destroy a myth to do so. i am all for certain kinds of destruction, natural. it's the only way to get anywhere when there is nowhere to get to but here. and anyway, who can destroy a myth who can destroy the kernel of its truth the trurh of its desire the desire of its being

ISRAELI AIR FORCE STRIKES GAZA TARGETS AFTER ROCKETS FIRED AT BE'ER SHEVA

ohtah: in the tensionspace nothingness devours being a god-given miracle of revelation to a people in love with time who celebrate the turn of each season with the corn and the wine wrought forth from the covenant with the seed-mystery

ohtoh: say that this is the last moment you had on earth to say something entirely earthly. would you say that the whatever of death is nothing compared to the grandeur of living? the grandeur of the incomprehensibility of living. would you say that the being of living is grander than the ineffability of dying. would you say that even after this moment your greedsoul would cling to living until it yields up its sacrilegious its devout envy its grandeurpassion. would you say that everything worth saying must be said even the most worthless the most vain prayer uttered in the fragments of the templestones parched of legends absent of myths the most altruistic flowering absurd song of itself

ohtah: so. we have to take up this question. it was supposed to be "what is a jew" but now it's become "what is here?" it's gone from a possible question to a non-sense question. a question that has wrought chaos with the senses. is that the transition the transformation from talmud to kabbala? from jesus christ to st. augustine? from shakespeare to beckett? from tanach to palmach? from what you were to what you are? to what you are not? so then: what is "are" and what is "are not"

ohtoh: he holds *the will to change* in the palm of his drained-out breath. It capitulates to the trembling that comes from the river. It resides in the miracle that we call the oscillations of the nerve ends. The trembling of *the will to change* recapitulates the birth from the womb. the stasis of pure action is a bloodtrust bridge to the action of pure thoughtimage from the perpetuum that illuminates the spectrum of light

ohtah: the equation is also a form of words which defines a reality. there was once an equation of grain and an equation of the fortifications for the heart

ohtoh: and i've taken up a history of the equations of the middle east and i've drawn up a series of equations of the middle east all of which include in them equations of the cosmos because everything is related to everything and because you can't describe a utopia without describing the struggle to achieve it without describing the history – in immutable equations – of the failure of utopias

AND THE FORECAST IS....HOT!

ohtah: is it possible to draw an equation of the mind?

ohtoh: it's possible to construct an equation of the history of the mind

ohtah: the individual mind or the history of mind itself?

ohtoh: isn't it im/possible to differentiate an equation of the landscape from an equation of the mind? doesn't every equation of a landscape signal an equation of the mind? an equation of wishes. an equation of detritus. an equation of knowing. an equation of personal objects.

UNITED STATES ATTACKS TALIBAN-HELD AFGHAN TOWN

ohtah: isn't every equation a book whose narration is finally pinned fully to the page and whose formulation has to be rewritten continuously.

ohtoh: here in the middle east we say the equation changes every ten minutes.

ohtah: even the name middle east is an equation. the equation is always asking: where am i/who am i

DANCE REVIEW: AVI GOTHEINER

ohtoh: the equation is always asking: what is change what is chaos what is the equation of the irrational *ohtah*: what might ever formulate the equation of the distance between us, between you and i

ohtoh: is there a distance between us, between you and i

ohtah: it depends on how you read the equation

FATAH ACUSSES IRAN OF TRYING TO BLOCK PALESTINIAN UNITY

ohtoh: you need an equation to define what you are and where your enemies are

ohtah: you need an equation to calculate that which lies at the heart of equation: the square root of the garden of eden divided by the faces of all buddhas of all times

ohtoh: an equation of delusions

ohtah: an equation of the odors of thought

CAN SHE LEAD?

ohtoh: an equation of sleep

ohtah: an equation of oppositions

ohtoh: at the heart of the same equation, then, there is gehenna, there is hell which is the garden of discord which is the anguish generated in the dissolution of ash into hate an inextinguishable flood remorseless in acid

ohtah: an equation of human energy

THREE NEO-NAZI PARATROOPERS SUSPECTED IN FRENCH SHOOTING

ohtoh: an equation of energy itself which is made of energy itself

ohtah: an equation of the human condition. doesn't every human have her/his own condition? make her/his own condition? *know* her/his own condition

ohtoh: i have seen written the equation of the leagues of friendship

ohtah: have you ever seen written the equation of the most wild sensibility of the desert

FOR PALESTINIANS, NON-VIOLENCE PAVES THE PATH TO STATEHOOD

ohtoh: i have seen written the equation of tender friendship

ohtah: and have you ever seen written the equation of the villages of pleasing verses

ohtoh: i have seen written the equation of the gallant letter

ohtah: and have you ever seen written the equation of the land of tendernesses

OBAMA OFFERS CONDOLENCES AS TOULOUSE STAND-OFF CONTINUES

ohtoh: i have seen the terms of the equation swirl both in fixed orbit and at random at every variable speed and on each plane of each universe alternative or other-wise

ohtah: have you seen the equation of the prophesy of the end of time

ohtoh: the equation of the end of time mirrors the equation of war & peace

ohtah: have you seen the equation of the concrete streets

YOEL SILBER TAKING ON DANCE MUSIC ESTABLISHMENT IN TEL AVIV

ohtoh: i have seen the complex equation which describes moses going through the city dressed as a beggar to see the people ascending as descending on the colored air collected from human breath made into art at peripatetic rituals

ohtah: what's the equation for the relationship between the animal the vegetable and the mineral including the horse but exclusive of the disorthodox teacher of ecstasy of joy rising and flying

ohtoh: i have seen written the equation of those lost in the lake of indifference;;;; those climbing the steep inclination to the hill of amity

ohtah: and do you believe what you see written

US LAWMAKER RELEASES HOLD ON AID TO PALESTINIANS

ohtoh: i believe that it's written. is that enough

ohtah: in a world where the word enough is a term of inquisition

ohtoh: for a time, i followed all the laws. each and every one of them. all the laws having to do with personal behavior; all the laws having to do with prayer and worship and ritual; all the laws having to do with transactions and justice; all the laws having to do with the harmonies of nature. i got more confused. i got entangled in a net of laws until the net became the only law and it had to be destroyed it had to be broken asunder even if what lay ahead was freedom and i didn't understand freedom

ohtah: is the book itself the book of lies? the book of puzzles? the book of lifetimes of beautiful and enigmatic letters

A NEW ADVENTURE

ohtoh: let's get back to some kind of reality, no? an equation of the peace of the middle east would do

ohtah: reality? that's a funny word to play with. it's the only word that wants to be itself that wants to be what it names

ohtoh: today i begin a new life. i construct it from the pantomime of leather and flax. from oil. from the chance meeting of an ohtoh and an ohtah, a him and a her. the foreordained correspondence of the mediterranean gods Gravitas & Levity

ohtah: let's begin a discourse that will have no end throughout the generations: let's begin with a court of analysis into the guilt *and* the innocence of the words "new" and "life"

PLANNED NUMBER OF IRON DOMES CAN'T OFFER FULL PROTECTIONS

ohtoh: while even birth isn't even the beginning

ohtah: drop it. the only thing that might follow this dialogue between ohtoh and ohtah is a question whose answer belongs to someone else, neither to ohtoh nor to ohtah. whose number is an equation beyond our mathematical beyond our astronomical abilities and belonging to the realm of the harmonies of science and poetics

ohtoh: and what about peace

ohtah: and what about peace

ACT SAFELY ON NEW YEAR'S EVE SO YOU CAN ENJOY 2012!

ohtoh: and what about life

ohtah: and what about life

SUNBODY

your body
is the sun
whose flame
burns
on the lips
of everyone
you kiss
you kiss your son
on his forehead
that kiss leaves a mark
mirrors read to him
every day
and then
rain pours down

until you will die
and your son
will cover all
the world's
mirrors with black
cloth
in mourning
when
he removes
the cloth the mirrors
are empty
but
for the moving angle
of the sun's reflections

i plunged
into
my son's room
to look
into his mirror
it blinded
me
so that i crawled
to my son
only he
could restore my sight
so i might see him
clearly enough
to offer my blessing
and wait
just to see
could he
receive it
without which blessing
he told me
he would walk
blinded
on this world's
glass

my father had given me
a horse
i rode it
to the
exhaustion
of wind

when i gave this same horse
to my son
he cursed me
saying there was no wind
left for him
to ride on
he rode that horse
on the very dessicate
absence
of wind laughing in
defeating me
and then he climbed down
off the horse
to see me
face to face

at the intersection
of the two words
we embrace in such a way
that our two
bodies will never
forget
the other
embodied
in the
human abyss
together

i told my son
i rejoice

in knowing you
in a way you will never
rejoice in knowing
yourself but
when, someday,
you swim in a waterless
sea
knowing yourself
you will rejoice
in a song titled
Where My Has Father
Gone

i
am your father
therefore i
am your legs
and i
am
inside them
only so that you
might outspeed me
in running headlong
over the edges
of obstacles
born of ancient
despairs

i handed over to you,
son, all the formed traditions
i knew

that had led our
forefathers toward
their gods
you renewed them
walking
across one bridge
only to return
over the same
water
by a different bridge
and then
over
the next bridge
and the next and
the next and the
next in a flight
from pain
i watched
but i wasn't allowed
to tell you you had already
gotten closer to god
than any of us
had done and that what i
could do was to watch
your flagrant
failures
open in your formless
ecstasies forming
languages with no
words to impede them

i gave you the gift
of a horrible
alienation
from life itself
i had to wonder
had i done it for the
perverse
pleasure of seeing you
struggle
to survive
to connect
with all the powers
of transient life
itself
i can't answer myself

please ask me
so that at that instant
of only your
asking
can i know
that
i will know
my own transient answer
flickering

do you remember
when you walked home
from school
naked
in the rain

through the sea
and you told me
that day you'd learned
to read. don't, i begged you,
look for me
in the books i've written
but it's too late you told me
you'd already found me there

don't you remember
yesterday you were
in the bathtub washing
off the water
and from where i stood
shaving
in the mirror
when, turning to you
i saw
and i said
good for you,
you're growing hair
down there
how horrified i was
to see shame
burn
the face
of my son
i tore
the heart out of
a lion
and i fed it

to you. and, even so,
the lion leapt
away, running
through the heart
of the sun
to burn off
the heat
of the human
and even though i
warned you
against
chasing
after it you
did so
what i could do
was to make an offering
to pretend gods
to protect you
where i
no longer could
you walked home
from that journey also
naked
in rain
and when i saw you
you came drenched
with sunwater

because your mother was not
in the room
when you were born

i offered her the sole right
to name you
when she told me
that when
you named your self
we would know about it even
if you named yourself
Water or Sky
or Earth
Ocean or Bird
or Fish
or Beast
No One or
Everyone or
Everything
The Unnamable or
Unnamed or even God

i gave birth to you
you
came from my body
in awe at the fact
of birth
and you
cut
your own
umbilical cord
skillfully

you will someday
hear me say

to you
but you will hear it
in your voice, inside your head,
in a language
of your design
and intimacy,
you will hear me say,
once
you are pure
even in your own
divine
uncertaintities then
i will return
to you and then
along with your
mother
will we dance
at the same
moment
as tragedy
comes
to the end of it
and dances
with her lover,
lyric,
as music
in the dancehall

once, when you were
an infant
you cried out

in hunger
and we fed you
and you slept
that same night i
woke up frightened
my body
so full
of an anxiety
i jumped
running throughout
the fields
of my hungry body feeding
my hungry mind with hunger
at the precipice of your
dream
where i watched you
breathe the breath
of the secret sky
i asked myself
who is it
who is so hungry
your dream
sang me
to sleep
filled
with your dream
where the candle went out
burnt to the end of
our light
where we slept
in our darkness

until the beginning
of time
when the universe
was void
and without any
form
at all
displayed
before us

i watched you
make an offering
of fire
to the fires that follow
i watched you make an offering
of gratitude for those moments
when you can close your
eyes on the flames
of rest
i watched you make a burnt
offering
of ash for the bonfire
of delusions
the delusions of fire i have watched
you make an offering of ash
to the ashes
revealing new
forms
i have watched you
make an
offering of knowledge

an the steps of
libraries on the steps of the
museum of the book
and go yourself bereft
of knowledges in search
of the origins
of flame
i have seen you come
to the edge of the fire
unable to jump in
and then to jump
in an offering of fireworth
washing
you through
your body down
to fire-quenched bones
i have watched you
make an offering of sky to
the earth
of grass
to the meadow
of my face
to your love
i bury my mind
in your lap
because you lead us
from the wilderness
into the wind

some say the storybook ends
with the death of the storyteller,

moses. some say it goes
on into joshua's wars are
life in the promised land of milk
and i say it goes on right here
with all of us
who bear the absence
of storyteller moses
in our words
where we conduct
our wars consume
the nectar
of our eyes in seeing
the fig tree in our
visions of feasts
of tea and wine

I took you
into the woods
to show you desire
you showed me the tree
that would haunt
all
of your
defeats in life
except
for your defeat
at the hand of mercy
and love at the beast
of your eternal
lustfevers
where you gave

yourself over
prisoner
of wisdom
you took me to
touch the one tree
that each night
rocked you
to sleep with its melodies
of silence
you showed me the
garden of treefaces
you had so feared
until they released you
into freefalling nowheres
of bliss
I saw the great tree
where your greatest
tree-chase had ended
in your weeping
of tree
we walked
until you took
my hand
to know its trembling
on the edge
of our days
which will be
my tree-gift
that fills your eyes
as they open directly
into your mindcalm of

real trees
every day
of every year
of your life
you took me
to the tree
you knew
as the tree
of hunger
you asked me
what pain should
you nurture
i told you
only one
will lead you
to the nowhere
to discover
it was your
country
and it was your
hunger
and you will clothe it
in myth and you will
anoint it
with rosewater

the kike from jew street

So in walks this Black dude with his buddy the Kike from Jew Street and I look up cause I'm washing glasses and I says who the hell are you two even though I knew for sure I knew em both what I'm not blind deaf and dumb you know I seen em both on the street a hundred times but they never come into my place before I figure they know better and I think well either they don't know better or they're tryin ta yank my chain and then I think you're not just off the ship yesterday so I go over to the other end of the bar to move the baseball bat closer to me and to give the little snipes a peek at it and they see it I know they see it, especially the Black dude who's not a small guy not at all and I know he's been around the block you can tell that on a Black dude and I don't care what the price of his shoes or the cut of his cloth which the Jewboy probably bought for him anyway and you watch he's the one who'll pay for the bill the Kikes what gotta always look like they got the dough whether they do or they don't whoa what's this coming in the door the Black dude's squeeze is who and she's the real ghetto too tight ass and just as tight a snatch don't you know so up the trio sashays up to the bar like a ménage a trio I'm tellin ya and the Black dude he orders up three Glenlivet - 25! - two on the rocks and one neat for himself. So I looks em over, the three of them there, waiting for their fancy-ass drinks, and I says OK, I says, it's on the house and I'll toast to you three myself. And when I got the glasses up, a neat for myself, and I make a toast like this I knew a Jewish guy once nice real nice guy you know got himself in trouble with the mob. Fed the poor sonofabitch bastard the Jew to the fishes. After which they come in here to celebrate. I'd seen em in here before. Tell me they like to come in here every time they have a celebration. And then one of em says to me, you know what he says, he says today we're celebrating a birthday and I says who's and the mobster he says Adolf's birthday, Adolf Hitler's. And they all laugh and of course I laugh with em. Then I stopped and we all were quiet for a second, for more than a second, looking each other over. Then the Jewboy breaks the silence and he says, I knew Adolf Hitler. Damned quiet after that. Nobody knew what the fuck to say then. Then the Black squeeze she says if my friend Amotz here says something, he doesn't fool around. Now what kinda Kikey fuckin Raghead name is Amotz? Amotz, I'm askin ya. And I got my hand wrapped round the bat. Where? I challenges the wise-ass little bastard. Where'd you know Adolf Hitler? In Auschwitz, Amotz says. Don't ask, the squeeze says again. I coulda wrapped those long black legs around my back I tell ya. So what can I do with that kinda sass but I says what you doing in whereverAusch with fuckin Adolf fuckin Hitler. Don't ask, Black Beauty says. Then Amotz himself he says real casual but real serious to me he says, if you truly want to know I'll tell you. Kinda shut me up he did, and not many people ever shut me up, I'll tell you that. And I see that guy Amotz, he's sitting there with his eyes closed now. He looks goddamn peaceful, you know, like he's got something I ain't got. Some kinda peace or some kinda power I ain't ever seen. I relax. My grip on the bat loosens. It even falls, leaning up against the bar. OK, I says to him, so OK so yeah I truly want to know. Opening his eyes, kinda slow, adjusting to the light of a bar in the afternoon, empty but for the three of them and me. He's sizing me up. Then he starts in: Auschwitz, he says, in Poland, was an extermination camp. Hitler sent people there, most times crowded into cattle cars. From the day it opened to the day it finished over a million maybe a million and a half of us died there in those gas chambers. Amotz stopped. He closed his eyes. I'd heard about all that shit, but a lot of people said it never happened, said the goddamn Jews made it all up. How'd I know? I didn't really care, tell you the truth. When Raghead opens his eyes this time, he's a different man. I don't know. I can't explain it. Still a Jew. But a difference. He goes, I arrived in Auschwitz on June 14th 1942. June 14th, he repeats it. Like what? Like I can't hear? I hear fine. It was a chaos of the demigods, he goes on, the stench of bodies burning. Smoke rising from the chimney. They put me to work. All day everyday daylong there is screaming. The guards, some of them, they like to pick on kids, 8 – 10 – 12 year olds – the little ones. The first time I saw them beat a kid with billy clubs I threw up. Then I stood there crying, sobbing. Those two guards saw me, heard me, looked over and came toward me. The kid runs away. No matter what happened to me I don't care the kid runs away. It happens again. Then again. Then again. Now, I'm known as The Weeper of Auschwitz, the Savior of Children. Here, he stops. He's exhausted. I'm spinning…is this guy for real? Who cares? What's real? In my bar at 3:30 in the afternoon, whatever you say, if you say it right, it's real. I thought he would start crying. He didn't. He was saying it just right. One day, he says, they haul me out into the yard, two big soldiers. One on the left one on my right. And there's Adolf Hitler, Adolf Hitler. They walk me over to him, and he says to me: Cry. I can't cry. The Füerher told you to cry, one of his aides, pistol in my face, says to me. You better cry. But Adolf Hitler, he says, No. Leave him alone. Bring me a boy. No! I beg Hitler. Don't do this thing! And the tears howl from my eyes! And like God begging man, the tears and the wailing arise double and triple and more from my eyes and my mouth. It's too much for me. I weaken. I fall on my knees to the ground. Adolf Hitler puts a hand on my right shoulder. Here. Right here. And Hitler says, to all assembled: don't touch this man. He is beautiful. A Jew is showing you pathetic excuses for Aryans how to be a man and what are the depths of mankind. I love this man. He is one of my treasures. Tomorrow, you will shoot him. He can live tonight in a greatest beauty, the tears of his own death. And that, Amotz says to me, is how I knew Hitler. In Auschwitz. I didn't ask Amotz how he got away. It didn't matter. He was telling me the truth. So I walked around the bar and I faced him and he stood up and I think he thought I was going to throw him out of the place, my place. And the truth is I didn't know what I might do. The baseball bat still behind the bar. My pistol in its niche by the sink. and I stood there and in front of Mr. Black Man and his high-horse Black Lady, I cried. I was a frightened little boy, myself. Mr Weeper of Auschwitz was saving me and my white ass. I couldn't stop. My guts were crying. My mind was crying. Christ my fuckin imagination and my momma were crying in me clawing to get out through my eyes. Me, who never cried in my whole life for nobody or nothing. And here I was like crying for every little goddamn child on earth. The woman, she stands up and she puts her hand on my shoulder, just like Aldolf Hitler done to Amotz on Amotz's shoulder. A hundred more tears get released. Now what the fuck you doin sitting there reading my story and you not crying. I gave out my broken into heart here, revealed it to you as a gift. And I ain't won't never get it back. So what you doing? You too busy? Too shut up? This ain't no little TV show or nothin. Cry, you. Cry for your life. I ain't crazy! If you can't cry with me now, you crazy you frozen you the one let them kids get beat up and killed. And who am I? Now I'm a kid what gets beat up and killed that's what.

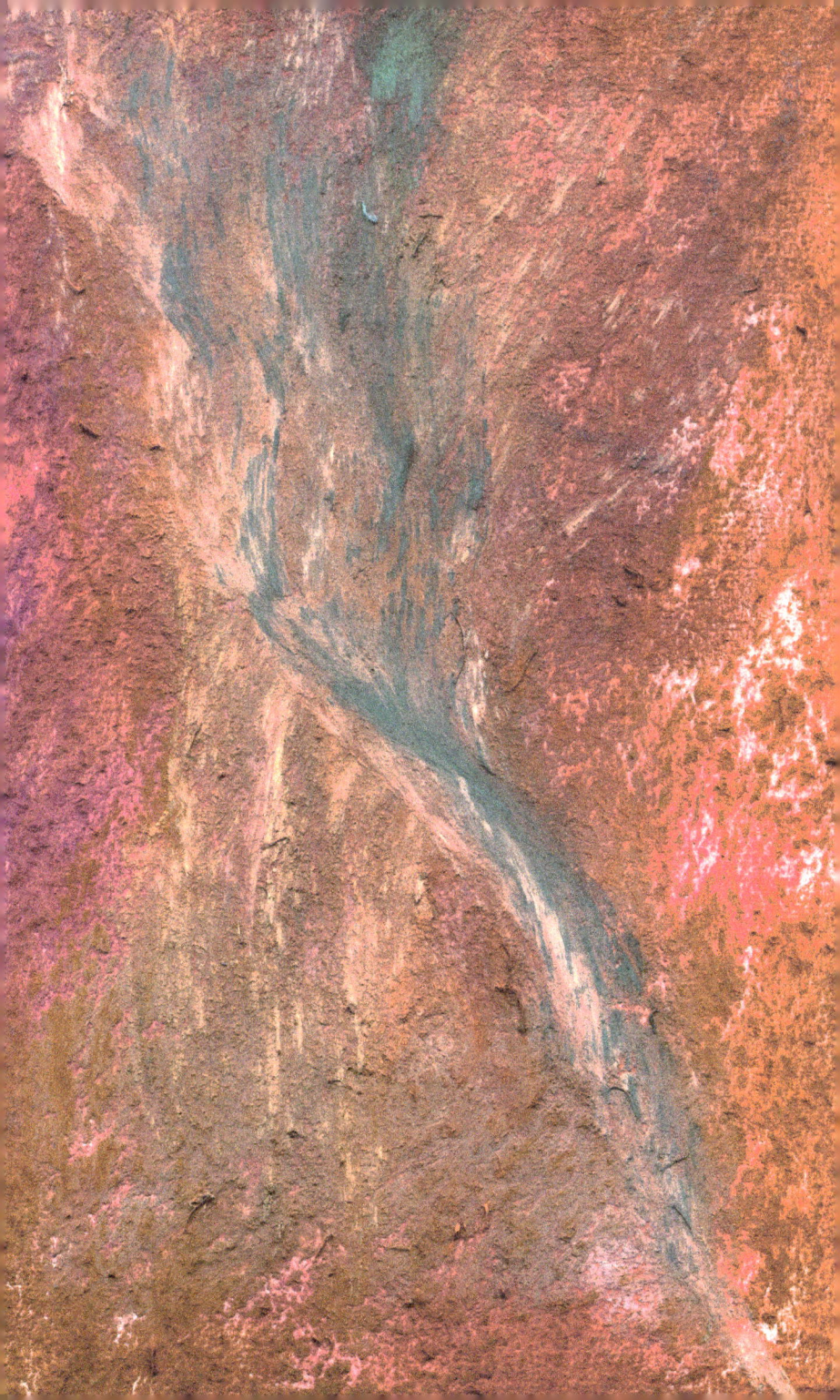

a reverie on fire & water
at a breach in a door of time

Did you drink the cup of water today?

Yes, I did.

Did you blow out the candleflame today?

Yes. I did.

Did you, today, in a restaurant, walk down the hallway to the men's room as a man walked past you on your right?

Yes, I did.

Did you plant two olive trees in your mother earth today?

Yes, I did.

Did you say to Noam today you always knew it could happen here, in our country, this fascism – fascism on the right and fascism on the left?

Yes, I did.

Did you visit with your grandfather at the cemetery today?

Yes, I did.

Did you go see the traveling circus today, the one run by zebras and fringees?

Yes, I did.

Did you meditate today?

Yes, I did.

Did you, today, as you walked down the hallway in the restaurant, hear a voice say to you, about the man who passed on your right: "Don't fear him"?

Yes, I did.

Did you climb a ladder today to discover it led nowhere, leaned up against nothing?

Yes, I did.

Did you open your arms today, gathering in all the children ever separated from their parents and families at our border with Mexico – to return them to whom and to where they belong?

Yes, I did.

Did you go, today, sign the papers to commit your Grandfather to Ypsilanti State Mental Hospital, then wait with him until the requisite two policemen arrived?

Yes, I did.

Did you feed the cat today?

Yes, I did.

Did you put your life on the line today?

Yes, I did.

Did you invent neologisms today to express what your language could not?

Yes, I did.

Did you enter the men's room in the restaurant today to find the man who'd passed you on your right in the hallway standing at the urinal, his back to you?

Yes. I did.

Did you wake up this morning, then erase the *tabula rasa* within you?

Yes, I did.

Did you drive into a storm today, heedlessly but carefully, skillfully?

Yes, I did.

Did you get a letter from Gary today that took your breath away, as always his handwritten letters do, with the flow of his ironic & his faithful & his passionate prose?

Yes, I did.

Did you go to relax today the Roosevelt Mineral Baths, with Bill and Tod?

Yes, I did.

Did you hear the man standing at the urinal in the restroom who'd passed you on the right in the hallway in the restaurant, say to you: "Don't cry"?

Yes. I did.

Did you plug in your earphones today, recharging them to listen to more of the audiobook of the Book of Isiah to fill in the lacunae in your reading, and in particular, your Biblical reading?

Yes, I did.

Did you see the prophet Ezekiel today, hiding in the bushes as you walked to work?

No, I didn't.

Did you listen to Peter Eötvos today?

Yes, I did.

Did you plan dinner tonight at Francoli's?

Yes, I did.

Did you, when the man standing at the urinal with his back to you in the restroom who'd passed you on your right in the hallway of the restaurant, said to you: "Don't cry," realize he had a gun?

Yes, I did.

Did you make cappuccino this morning for yourself, your wife, and your father-in-law?

Yes, I did.

Did you respond today to the invitation from the Israeli Consulate for the showing of the film about White Supremacism at the Museum of Tolerance?

Yes, I did.

What did you wear today?

I chose light blue jeans, a warm light-grey Tommy Bahama pullover that my mother-in-law had given me, with my black Puma Roma tennis shoes.

Did you clean the house today?

Some, yes, I did.

Did you write this poem today?

Yes, I did.

Did you contemplate that image of Cezanne's today?

Yes, I did.

Did you make eggs for your wife today, as your cat meowed, rubbing up against your leg?

Yes, I did. I did.

Did you today, at lunch, feel tears in the core of your mind that wait unwept?

Yes, I did.

Did you see your wife today, tired, but work nonetheless in her way, dedicated to her work, to her students?

Yes, I did.

Did you, when everyone had left the house this morning, walk around to and fro, from room to room, reveling in the warmth of sunlight that came in from the small and the big windows?

Yes, I did.

Did you talk to me today?

Yes, I did.

And who am I?

Did you know that in northern Italy, Michaelangelo designed and planted a wild garden that is still there?

Did you see a rose today, when you visited Wallace Stevens?

No, I didn't. And yes, I did.

Did you see the River Nile flood today, overflow its banks?

Yes, I did.

Did you own your death today.

Yes, I did.

Your birth?

Even so.

Even so as the two are one?

Even so.

Nameless?

Even so.

Did you have wonderful conversations with your students today?

Yes, I did.

Did you see today your father's tank Commander in Germany, in WWII, gone insane, jump off the deck of their Sherman tank, break his neck?

Yes, I did.

Did you read Rimbaud today, where he writes: J'ai un autre; I is an other?

Yes, I did. And more poems of Rimbaud and Robert Creeley and Abba Kovner and William Carlos Williams and watched films by Robbe-Grillet and Truffaut and Bergman and Elon Indursky and Julia Loktev.

Yes, I did.

Did the man in the restaurant at the urinal with his back to you who'd passed you on your right as you walked down the hallway in the restaurant pull the trigger?

No. He didn't.

Did you have a piece of the date nut bread that Rebecca bought for you before you left for work today, with cream cheese?

Yes, I did.

Did you catch the odor of citrus from your kumquat tree today when you left for work?

Yes, I did.

Did you love anyone today?

Yes. I did.

Did you breathe today?

Yes. I did. I did breathe.

mind

in the penumbra
of the infant-
mind
comes without
prelude comes
an eye
of light
comes a voice
of song
comes absence
comes caverns
of isolation
comes the birth
of signs
turning
the infant-mind
backwards
and forwards to
vast
continents
of being of
love
and of betrayals
unnameable
which we call
the panic
of man's
desiring
and open

our arms
to
a cup
of tea
to a sip
of falling
with nowhere
to land
but into
the body
of the infant-
mind hurling penumbrae
in your direction watch it! they sur-
round
you   in-
       fuse you they
become you it happened
once to me & now
i know who i is and in what
seas
to swim

        in this swirl
        of creatures fallen of legends
        i greet you i am the genius
        of water i am the light of
        shadows i invite you here
        on this playground to
        stand in the equivocality of my
        beating heart to flesh of my
        poise to bone of my

        enigmaticity
        together we constitute one
        choir of hallelujah
so thank you
    sir and
thank you
ma'am you
can buy me a stiff
one when we meet all the others
wherever in monastic hell
or heaven they gather to
drink inside the end
of hallucinations
and other decorums good/bye goodbye
and goodbye forged universal
time

lust

after
i'm gone
forget
me
as already i have
forgotten myself
to live
in the world
as it is
in awe
of every kind
to live
in the house
of study
in awe
of every
kind
when i'm gone
forget me as you
forget
yourself
in awe
of every kind

when i'm gone
forget
your empty
memory where we
are dancing
and you
teach

the earth
to soil

my empty memory
where i create
universes
of bread
of hunger
of galaxies
of awe

when i'm gone say kaddish
for yourself invoke
my invocation
of the living
to the living
of every kind
for everyone throughout
galaxies
of bread of
light of time
for everything
after I'm gone
share
      my human-born
lust
      for the light-pierced
        body
          of silence
with

energy

buildings collapse. houses collapse. skyscrapers. skies collapse. doorframes. police stations collapse. garden sheds collapse. monuments collapse. churches collapse. trees collapse. church towers and bell towers collapse. hospitals collapse. hills collapse. mountains collapse. seas collapse. valleys collapse. families collapse. democracies collapse. fortunes. walls collapse. machines collapse. baseball parks collapse. stars collapse. words collapse. Philosophers
                        collapse. emotions collapse. empires collapse. modernity collapses. private property collapses. consciousness collapses. the marriage of time & space collapses. sponge cake collapses. memories collapse. psychic structure collapses. currencies collapse. forests of trees collapse wars collapse. collapse. grand stairways collapse. earthquake collapses. solar storms collapse. hurricanes. floods. delusions collapse. metaphors collapse. magnetism collapses. numbers collapse. sundays. mondays, wednesdays, yesterdays – collapse. fire collapses. the abyss collapses. missing you collapses. hatred collapses. peace collapses.

it

the white
pebble-stone loves me.
the twig branch
loves me
the seashell
loves me.
the flower vase and the candlestick love me
love is air
and air loves me
love moves faster
than light
and light loves me
there is no unified theory
of the universe
in physics
and theories and universes and physics
love me
the word loves me
glass loves me
and sand loves me
paper and electricity love me
the ice-moon in
the day sky and
the night sky loves
me
and time loves me
it's inevitable
inevitability
loves me

songs and poems love me
magnets and compasses
love me
chairs
love me
the waters above and the
waters below and the
ships that sail on them
love me
        the rain
loves me wind
loves me there is no
time outside of time
rhubarb
loves me and tomatoes
and mushrooms love me
the body
of my mother
loves me my
father loves me
daughters and brothers
sisters and basements and
attics love me beds
and bedspreads windows love me
cars
love me elephants
love me
houses love me waterfalls
gardens and grain silos
love me
the grass loves me

the spoon and the fork and the cup
they all like the coffee
and the tea love me
like the crows
the crows do
they do every of them loves me
and the sparrows
and the movies
and the poems
love me california and nevada and michigan and
new york
and paris and denver and jerusalem
they love me from up close
and from the distances of space alone
does space also love me?
of course of course it does
even the sun loves me and neptune
and earth love me
sleep
loves me the
sidewalk
loves me my shirt and my pants
and my shoes love me
even my shoelaces love me
the light of day the night of light
they love me as the day itself and it is a day deep as
the night itself and it is in the deep depths of this deep
night that it
loves me loves
me loves me

abyss

the abyss

      it is a bright

white white

      light sus-

           pended

by a cord un-
anchored

         and wind
         a wind

as doors

A door opens. You walk through. You sit down in the one chair around. You wait. A door opens. You don't cross the threshold. Inside, you encounter a man sitting in a chair. Waiting? He might bear your memory. You step back. The door won't close. You don't laugh, but you smile – gently – as if to yourself, but only as if. A door opens. You want to go through. You step. You have one foot on either side, as it were, as it were. Over the threshold. There need be a going forward there need be no turning around. When your mother arrives, you talk about things, about what is happening in the world. When you ask her her name she doesn't laugh but smiles – gently – at you. A door opens. No, not quite. A door opens. It won't close. Something pours forth. It pours forth. You don't know what it is. The Waiting Man knows. Your question to him is this: Will you tell us? A door opens. You cross the threshold. You sit in the chair that waits for you. You see this is not yourself. You see this is everything of yourself. When your father arrives, he says to no one but you, "is this all there is?" "red, you answer, red red red red." He asks you again, "Is this all there is?" A door opens, he enters across the threshold. When a fierce wind arrives, you repeat yourself, speaking as if – but only as if – to no one, "Red. Red red red." A door opens. A stranger sits at a writing desk. He writes: "Red red red red." You open a door. Your grandmother and grandfather make love in a room of no bed no walls no ceiling. You open a door. Your father and mother make love in a room of no bed no walls no ceiling. … their passion for each other, their desire for you. You are born into this world of no doors no walls. You wail. Your father says to you, "Red red red red!" Your mother names you All-There-Is.

dinner

...and there we were and we had come because it had been rough those days and you'd started writing again after that long hiatus that hit you when your mother died. and there we were and, after talking for quite a while with the sommelier whom we'd just met about all those wines in the wine case, and there they were those german tourists that young couple he an art historian of 19th century stained glass windows and she a doctor at the hospital in munich and you talking loudly over the din of the restaurant and I wondered were you doing it so they the german couple would hear and because that was just after your father had remarked: there they are on vacation a lovely german couple and here we are three american jews and isn't it all just too crazy and such a waste and so stupid all those wars, because you at that table where we sat right there by those doors open to the sea at sunset I'd thought much like our wedding sixteen years ago this time of evening that kind of sky over that ocean the pacific ocean about just 40 miles north of here and you working on this novel now which led you to what you'd been talking about for a few years anti-semitism and war and your grandfather's old diary from wwI that you wanted to incorporate into your book and that today or yesterday I think it was you discovered online at brigham young university library a book an actual history of your grandfather's unit the 77th engineers company in france in a field of shelling and mustard gas and hiding in a cave and then when the sea below threw up that hugh breaking wave that shuddered the three of us anyway into a moment's silence of awe and looking at each other and looking at that sea out there from which we were so safe and then you went on talking to your father about his father all of which I was listening to but had talked with you all day about so I was drifting in my mind thinking wwI 1918 where were my grandfathers my mother born 1919 her father having just immigrated over from England my father born 1917 his father having come a while earlier so the holocaust and that war and those germans at the next table did they have an ear to us to these american jews and did they have anything in germany no it's landlocked anything like this this immense and immensely overpowering sea three, four foot waves breaking at high tide right up to the seawall beneath us at the hotel restaurant and I saw those two young 28 maybe 30, 32 year old women stop at the seaside where we'd walked earlier, where they paused, where they then and together walked into that grey and blue and greenly sea why? and then I turned my full attention back to you and your father talking about his father us all picturing joe there in eastern france hobbling with his broken ankle carrying a fellow soldier out of the cave and the woods on his back then hit himself in the back of his neck with shrapnel that sent him to the hospital so that it wasn't long then we were talking and the helicopter made its first low pass close now to us and to that now violent violent sea and as it made its second pass close down over our heads and the hotel patio out the door just behind you when you and I looked at each other and it went on and more and more people watching that helicopter and buzzing and watching the now you could see in its dark color its very coldness its awful turbulence and when we talked a bit to each other about it and to our waitress and the woman at the concierge desk who told us how to go online to find news about it at the local newspaper so that when we walked down that corridor you'd said to me if it's what everyone thinks it is, surely, at least, its over by now and she's dead and drowned or he is or they are because I can't stand to think of her or him or them in that moment of nakedness of spirit in the midst of that sea in their terror and then after a long quiet ride up the coast I said I don't think I'm being selfish and I don't think I'm a just a voyeur thrill-seeker here but I'm strangely glad we were here tonight because I am with them out there I am human and they were human and fragile and terror-stricken and small in our nature of a sea here and I am with them and I feel that and I am glad to bear witness here to what must be.... for them..." And we came home. I fed the cat. You called your father, who said to you: they had no business going out there with their deathwish into that sea at that hour of the evening, and I heard you, you said to your father: it's ok, you can feel for them, it won't frighten you too much tonight, and your father said, he said back to you: ok. but it will. thanks for showing me all that about my father. thanks for catching that phrase in his diary where he talks about being lonely. He didn't express emotion much. He was a quiet man that way, quiet and tough.

water

water
>is a nursing
>ritual
>>to the rising
>>of a human being
>>being human

water, created of one part hydrogen and two parts oxygen generated in the visionary dreams of pre-galactic alchemy when the galaxy was neither void nor dark

if adult humans are 55-60% water that is the genius of water in its transformation from alchemy in a great leap across millions of waterless eons to become human

every time we drink a glass of water we recreate ourselves in cycles of dessication/hydration of the cellular human consciousness

wars have been waged over water. this poem is a lifesaving draught of water i offer to each of my enemies right now. each one, drink, I say, with me.

no one has ever died for lack of the water on earth. millions have drowned under the curse of misaligned imagination

there are river-gods and there are sea-gods and there are thunder-gods and rain-gods. no culture yet has gone so far as to recognize the sea, the thunder, the rain and even the sun are all made of water. now, we come alive. we no longer fear to use our knowledge to create our unknowing, to invent the god of water, H2O, right now, in this poem.

this poem is made of water. it is read by water. it offers praise to water. it creates ceremonies of the brotherhood and the sisterhood of water.

water cleanses water. that teaches us how to heal all the waters.

a woman who dreamt she was drowning, awoke kicking, sucking breath. calming, she restored her state of deepest sleep – the water she had thirsted to drown in.

no force has ever succeeded in destroying water – not hate or fear or greed or narcissism or sexual violence or murder not self-destruction…no force has ever *not* needed, desired, thirsted for, loved water.

the water-god of water…is water. water in ceremonies of supplication prayer, awe-prayer to water. this is no tautology. it's not sophistry. it's not language games. it's not theosophy or theology. it's energy in our galaxy. it's not a form of vanity but of an abundance of being.

it's possible for a human to go 40 years with no water. and then drink, slowly. it happened, once. he became known as the Keeper of Faith. he died in new york city, on the lower east side, abject, penniless, revered. thousands hundreds of thousands attended his funeral in the Street of Water that goes down to the River

Milk is water
        whiskey
      is water
   tin & the veins in stone & glass
numeric equations are water

        thought is water &
            thoughts of water
      are water
                grass
                is water the trees
                    are water
           the sky the cloud the aether
           are water the pendulum is water
                new york, karachi are water
     judaism is water
     buddhism is water
     ceremony is water
        history
      geometry
      are water
truth is water
that truth of electricity in water

           the aura
           of the negotiations
           of dynamic balance
           between thought
           and no-thought
           is water

        the moment
        wherein no-thought
        embraces thought
        is water
are those moments re-
visited when we
see ourselves unable to cross the dark
watery chasms
of enveloping night is where we
see a love supreme. water? yes.

the sheen of time is water
the power of surrender is water

myth is all water,
the truth in it, its
waterwater

complete faith is water
complete doubt is water
completely the desire
to be known in
complete desire
is water

in the sovereign dominion of water there is no margin of
error you have nothing but trust to consume

in the realm of water the doors of secrets are washed away
everything personal is revealed

mother is water
father is water
brothers and sisters
families
are water gush
out surge forward
    from the water-source
    in no-origin

        aristotle is water
            spinoza and derrida
        are water
        einstein is water $e = \text{water} \times \text{water}^2$

water   drops
from the icicle
that hangs
from the eaves
at some
point
in the thousands
and eons
of eras
when the earth
turns an $n^{th\circ}$ sunward
the icicle melts altogether
temporarily
at some point
in the midst
of these passions
i fall in love

with you
we lie together
our eyes
open, aware
inside this watertime
that the icicle
is water
as well
as the sun
is water as well
our breath
as well
our sleep
are water
the word water
on the edge
of being spoken
fills
with water
to flowing
over
and to overflowing

because of hakuyu taizan maezumi roshi
a variation on his six words + one image

Q: what is the radiance of time
A: the radiance of time is light

Q: what do you - as a human being - need, to live
A: time

Q: of all the qualities of time, which is the most important
A: motion

Q: who invented time
A: energy

Q: what is the ritual of time
A: washing the body

Q: who is the recipient of time
A: sleep

Q: how do we measure time
A: in the pouring of the cupful of wine

Q: what is the potential of time
A: music

Q: what is the turbulence of time
A: chaos

Q: what is the behavior of time
A: eros

Q: what is the dream of time
A: consciousness asleep

Q: what is the lunacy of time
A: the lunacy of time is the dismantling of civilizations in the rising in the falling of the riverstides of order

Q: what is the lunacy of time
A: the lunacy of time is the aroma of time engaged with human lunacy with all its contradictions the flows of images even of the inversions of good and evil in resolute intimacy

Q: what is the lunacy of time
A: the lunacy of time is the irreversible radiance of light

Q: ok, really, now, what is the lunacy of time

Q: what is the relative perspective of time
A: the relative perspective of time is in that space which gives momentum to the revolutions of heavens and hells into a blur

Q: what is the purpose of time

Q: what is the meaning of
Q: what is the pleasure of time
Q: what is the logic of time

A: the logic of time
   is the irrational

Q: what is the irrationality
   of time
A: the irrationality of time is
   in your
   birth and in mine

Q: what is the teaching of time
A: the teaching of time is the art
   of communion

Q: what is the wound of time
A: the wound of time is the past
   the present
   and the future
   of love all of which
   happens only now

Q: what is the embrace of time
A: you   are the embrace   of time
   as am I

Q: what is the fulfillment of time
 A: the fulfillment of time is zero
    that zero which is not nothing
    and that nothing
    which fills continuously with the air
    between us

    overflowing the brim
    of zero

Q: what is the tragedy of time
A: the tragedy of time is
   not knowing time and not
   knowing that timelessness
   which we call not-time

Q: what is the comedy of time
A; the comedy of time is the marriage
   of time and sentimentality

Q: how does the body experience time
 A: the body experiences time in the 700,000,000
    births and deaths that occur
    in the blink of its eyes

Q: how does the mind experience time
A: the mind experiences time in the folding
   of time into time into time

Q: what is the absence of time

A: time neither
   slows down nor does it speed up

A: yes, time is real

A: time is not the god

    or the demi-urge
    that created the universe,
    nor that created good
    and evil

A: time is the timeforce that created time

A: yes.

A: yes.

A: yes.

BECAUSE OF TETSUGEN ROSHI
BERNIE GLASSMAN

amazing.
the world
is filled with air
and we breathe it
the world is filled
with cows with
months with days
of the week
with arms and with legs
with religion
with silverware
with hunger
the world is filled
with paper
it is filled with bread
with starvation
with drought
amazing!
the world
is filled
with yoghurt with peanuts
with grain
with wine
the world is filled
with grandmothers
with murderers
with feces
with urine

with good health
with napkins
with fine dinners
the world is filled
with art
with art
with artists
with evil
with dread
with coffee
with clocks
with martinis
with mailmen carrying packages
of cakes through the winter
steppes
from Odessa to Warsaw
the world is filled
with long blasts
on a ram's horn
the world is filled
with distance with
separation
it is filled with spring
and with deserts
and with chemicals
the world is filled with mouths
with ears hearing
thunder over the eighth sea
the world is filled
with those who bring

light
and the light that is
darkness with them

and the world is filled with envelopes
with sex
with communion
amazing!

the world is filled with marble
and with stone it is filled
with airplanes with
human insanity with
amazing!
it is filled
with uncertainty
with massive gulfs
of unknowing
it is filled
it is filled
with mind with image with
dreamscape with hotels with ice
and with black ice and
with ice-cream
although the world
is filled
with signs
and with meaning they
are each
and all of them subject

to change and so oh
yes
the world
is filled
with change or
no
the world is change
it is made
of the substance
of change what
after all
can we fathom
what world can we not
fathom we
who are

right now

in childhood – happening right now
on this turf of fertile plains
there is a field of wheat
he has fire
in his hands
a torch of fire
he doesn't burn
the field
he doesn't burn it
down

in childhood – exactly now
here in this lowland desert
there is a mother
there is a father
she knows them but they
have forgotten her
and who
she is
she dives further
and further
into who
she is not
with the courage of
trust

in childhood
high
in these cold mountains
there are the nights
of the three moons
of the seven stars
of the one planet four
billion
light-years away
there are the days
and the nights
of the one thing
he will forget
to be held in abeyance
until
he can return
to see it
led by the gift
of the genius
of his intellect led
by the guidepost
of his language
that leads him
into thickets
of invisible trees

in childhood – existing not then but now
deep in this
urban maze
there are moans she hears
from those around her

moans they dare not
mutter aloud
lest they hear themselves
she already knows
to just listen but
to the
intermittent flow
to her/self passion
in it all

in childhood
nowhere
every crevice
of extreme emptiness
fills
with contemplations
of betrayals
of colors
of elephants
of the books
from antiquities that question him
about abysses
about beings
and nothingness
there are errors
in all
of his answers
they are the
tools he has
to pry open
the powers

he inherits
into his flesh
and bones
from the forthpouring
of the truths
of reality
illuminated
in his dreams
implanted there
in the semen
of his grandfather's
enormously subtle
wisdom
left to grow
in the dark

in childhood – right here & now
in the heart of earthquake country
she sings already
the next
song the one
that obliterates
the last
song
in a carefully crafted
ritual
of abandon
and creation

in childhood – here, here,
you see, here,

where he grows
in the consciousness
of imagination
he makes the initiates'
first
love
to his first
young lover
on a train
of blue water
she who gently
declines with no
and no and no
to get off
the train
with him
but goes
on
and on and
on choosing
to be delirious
to be lost
 & lost &
consumed
in the haze
of the memory
of the long
and the heart-
felt and the melan-
choly Embrace of the Lost
he gave her

and
had left behind
for her
even as
he took it
with him

and then
in childhood
in the mirrorworld
where she grew up
she makes
sexual
love
to herself
where the conundrum
of birth and the breath
of life and the life
of it
and the rages
of love
marry all together
in that ceremony
called A Radical
Communion
With the Gift
of Silence

and then
he takes the fire
he had held

in the vast
field of his father's
wheat
to hold it up
to see into his
father's eyes
and through his
father's eyes so
far beyond
himself
there is
therein
no self left
and the fire goes out
and he sees
him and he kisses him

in childhood
now
at this
vertigo
of excess
wrought
on the edges
of latitudes
of longitudes
of wanderings through battlefields
of the homeless
until arrives
face
to face

where
no matter the age
of this earth
pressed up against the
flowing
water
of the last
wall
   are born
trailing
behind of it   of in
to honor
of it

protogenesis

precisely
at the crossroads
in the desert
on tuesday
where the pure
and the impure
collide
a fireball, which,
cooling:
the body
recapitulates
for the first
time the innumerable
laws of physics

variations on a leitmotif

…washing off the water with the salt.
revenge is achieved by the surprise appearance of untooled being
washing off the water with the sky.…

At the housing development turn what you always thought of as left
keep going until you arrive at the centerhouse
after entering the centerhouse go around the entire interior perimeter then go turn
again to what you think of as left
and keep going
washing off the water with the numbers

desire
      was the absence
her tongue whispering
an earth that never
 left us a

the end of violence hung on the baretree branch the knowledge of this is secreted through the pores into the whiplashed air coloring the sunset blue rivers of warplanes stream toward the youth of the homeland neither acceptance nor rejection accomplishes the wholeness of the wetborne day washing off the water with acid washing off the water with the color gold or the anthem blue this is the green world worth living for the world of glass in stone the world of thin men talking on telephones speaking in tongues the sleeping in the sleep which has neither interior nor exterior elevation the end of the line came they stepped off the water. where sensibilities had gathered under the baretree. an earth turns shaking off the water. a dry earth is not. the convocation of tenderness took place under the sky and all the participants were pieces of paper written on or infants carried in basketry. it will open and repeat. it will resist berlin and commodification. it will open and repeat. it will carry you the complete distance to the organism. washing off the water with the stillwater. washing off the water with the discovery and the naming of the theory of relativity. the correlation between safety and joy abides in both the absence and the presence of snow. standing in the fecund and thoughtless storm. cross the tundra without walking. examine the wind for spores of light. navigate the corridors of nothing at all that everything made of matter and the matter of mind.

washing off the water with the theory of the separation of water & fire.

learn to row backwards through the water into the city of beginnings in order to be surrounded by apparitions of freedom and the devil's choir of innocence

two

a darkness at a window word layered upon word a goodness of the heart a proliferation of time an outburst of noise a remembrance of a promise a spelling of the word word a layer of word upon an insistence of DAH DAH DUM DAH heard not in the mind but across the wires of the old telephone without the telephone itself to intervene oh you young outcast you crying by the flood of intellectuals collected at the corner of possible disruption of your silence we know who you are and who you were collecting individual breaths to form into a concerto then gathering all the instrumentations as musicians themselves never disconnected from the note up and along all the ethnomusical scales including those invented in other galaxies which must exist because the letter X exists in this galaxy written only with two straight lines overlapping at the strange interpenetration of heart and soul of gravity and suspension of the ancient and the now that conjunction as memorial of the big bang containing all matter in time and space a long drawn out vowel such as oooooooooooooooooooooooooooooooooo oooooooooooo
iiiiiiiiiiiiiiiiiiiiiiiiiiiiiiiiiiiiiiiiiiiiiiiiiiiiiiiiiiiiiiiiiiiiiiiiiiiiiii iiiiiiiiiiiiiiii uuuuuuuuuuuuuuuuuuuuuuuuuuuuuuuuuu uuuuuuuuuuuuuuuuuuuuuuuuuuuuuu not as repetition but in continuum

some lies about the birds of venice

alice monet

In Venice, Mme. Alice Monet wrote in her diary that the birds she heard on awakening each dawn – not the legendary flocks of pigeons, of course, but the plethora of other birds, the passerine – were like no other birdsong she'd ever heard. "I'm sure," she wrote, "that it's the influence of not only – but led by – the bell of Campanile di San Marco but from all the bells of all the bell towers gathering together. It's not coincidental that after centuries and generations of birds flying amid the bells these birds have absorbed the sounds into their bodies into their minds to the point where they magnificently have altered their own song. The birds, to some degree, are the bells, the bells, the birds. When I can't sleep, I imagine the birdsong I will hear again at dawn, until I do sleep, having become, in some degree, myself, the birds, the bells."

michel sambaque

An extensive, exhaustive study of birds world-wide reveals there may be as many as 500,000 species! In the early part of the 20th century, the aviarian, Michel Sambaque, embarked on an investigation to discover what effect the sounds of different birds' chirping had on different populations of people. Did certain birds have a calming effect, while other birds – an excitatory effect? Did certain birds make people think differently than did other birds? M. Sambaque began working in South America, intending to travel on every continent. After 16 months' work, he gave it up. He wrote in his diary: "It's not possible to arrive at any conclusions because there are far too many factors, too many variables. For example, how can you isolate, in Brazil, the effect of song of the incredible momotus momota from the effect of the forest itself. How, in Kenya, separate the effect of the song of the red-winged lark from the effect of the grasslands. How distinguish the influence of hunger from the influence of bird song."

M. Sambaque's friend, Georges Clemenceau, a friend also of the Monets, wrote to Sambaque about Mme. Monet's impressions of the birds of Venice. M. Sambaque quickly departed to Italy. In Venice, he took a room in the same hotel where the Monets stayed, the Barbaro Palace on the Grand Canal. On waking his first morning in Venice, he wrote in his notebook: "Mme. Monet was right. Looking back on it, every bird I've listened to over the last 16 months has a similar effect. If only you can listen, can learn to hear."

When M. Sambaque ran out of money an Italian friend, Michealangelo Venetiano, gave Sambaque a room in his Venice home. Unfortunately, that room was on the ground floor. When the canals flooded that year in their annual cycle, not only were some important papers of Sambaque's nearly destroyed, but Venetiano, in disgust, gave up this annual Venetian ordeal and left the city. Sambaque had no choice but to go home.

robert straud

My friend, Robert Straud, told me that the only regret in his life was that, after reading in Mme. Alice Monet's letters about the birds of Venice, he wanted desperately to go there, to wake up in the morning to hear the birds that Mme. Monet heard, but, of course, he couldn't. He told me that if he heard those birds, his life would be complete. Everything he'd suffered would be made tolerable. Well, first of all, I think he vastly overstated the case. No birdsong no matter how soft or how elegant can do that for you. But, more importantly, I asked him: Robert, that's your only regret? You don't regret murdering the bartender? Don't you regret murdering the prison guard at Leavenworth in front of eleven hundred prisoners? Don't you regret the brutality against others that got you years and years and years of solitary confinement, even if that confinement meant discovering the canaries? Don't you regret a life of violence and imprisonment? How can you so dishonor the victims of your violence by giving me this crap about not hearing the birds of Venice being your only great regret! You know what he told me? He told me: I didn't really murder anybody. Then he said: Did I? I didn't really murder anybody, did I? And I'll tell you what I think, Harold. I think that Straud dreamt somehow that he'd heard those birds of Venice and that birdsong – mad as this all is – erased the sins of his life for him. You know I found him so congenial, so sweet. But I didn't meet him until after the canaries. Yet, this delusion about the birds of Venice! But I'll tell you something. You go to Venice. You tell me what it's like. Because when I get out of here – and that'll be quite soon now, as you know, I'm going to Venice. You'll have to lend me the money. I'll pay it back. If I can begin my life of freedom after lo these many years of imprisonment with hearing those birds, then I'll make it the rest of the way. I'll be alright. Listen to me!

p.s. have you ever seen the Monets from his Venice sojourn? They're amazing. They'll make you smile and weep and evoke a quiet peace in you all at once. They have that kind of evocative possibility.

Letter, Johannes Vole, from Alcatraz
To Harold Levitsky

harold levitsky

The world is in fact a sleepy place. Everyone, at any given moment, could just let go and their bodies fall and find themselves wherever they are, lying down, asleep. It's a sweet thought; a sweetening image of being. There is a tribe in South America that acts of this reality. They sleep. They hunt, they cook, they eat, they have sex, they celebrate their rituals, and, in their hammocks, chewing on some mildly psychedelic plant root, they sleep. They sleep away mornings and afternoons. They sleep away evenings, and then, after ceremonies that exhaust them, they go in to bed. They sleep in peace, untroubled by anything but the most luminous of dreams. Even in dreams of violence, they are the victors: dreams of hunting, dreams of wars with neighboring tribes, dreams of violent ritual. So their dreams are never rattled by anything disturbing enough to interrupt their sleep. It's almost – not quite – but almost – as if, when they die, someone could put them in the hammock where they spent their life and there they would belong unto eternity.

I write about these people from my hotel room now at the Barbaro Palace in Venice because, as I'm about to go to the University to lecture on this tribe in Brazil, whom I studied, lived with, got to know intimately – the birds chirp outside my window. Do they remind me of the birds of Brazil? No. I don't think so. But their soft chirp has a soporific effect on me. I could just fall into my bed and sleep so happily. But. No. I am a civilized man. A scholar. I belong to a whole different culture from my people in Brazil. I have business to perform that has little to do with hunting or eating or sex. I have to go lecture to people who most likely will wish they could live like my Brazilian friends. They could go to their hammocks as I speak in that great hall. Or, they are the other kind. They will condemn my Brazilian tribe for their laziness, their slowness, their waste of their lives. Either way. I'll go shower, I'll dress. The sound of those birds here will drift only into the background of my day. Until, perhaps, if I wake up early enough tomorrow, I'll hear them. I have no obligations in the morning. Maybe I'll sleep in. But maybe not. Either way, I will not include in my lecture the experience of hearing certain members of the tribe in their sleep flawlessly replicate the birdsongs of the rainforest. For my protection and to shield the tribe.

blanche hoschedé monet

Mme. Alice Monet wrote to her daughter that in Venice the soft chirping of the birds at dawn was a powerful thing. A delicate power that entered into her sleep and that became a long moments' extreme soft deep fleeting but lasting pleasure when she awoke. Even, she wrote, when Monet despaired, finding his canvases ugly, finding that Venice was too beautiful to be painted, that it was untranslatable, Mme. Monet still – each dawn – was always heartened by the birds. Even if, she wrote, she arose always to fits of anxieties, the birds' soft chirping would mingle with those anxieties, not dispersing them, not even diluting them, but – as if molecule by molecule – displace them with their sonorous and radiant reality. If, she told Monet, I could translate those sounds into white lead, cadmium yellow, vermilion, madder, cobalt blue, chrome green – wouldn't that be as magnificent an oratorio as is a Monet canvas a magnificent vision. But mostly, she wrote, she was so happy to see Monet – once he found a way to come into it – so impassioned by his Venetian canvases as he moved around daily, following light. At least, she wrote, for the time being anyway, no more of those lilies! I love these Venetian paintings, she later wrote, from Givenchy, where Monet finished them, as the highest expression of his art. They are not Venice, she wrote. They are not the birds of Venice. They are Monet, transformed, as if alchemically, by Venice. There's a difference.

the birds of venice

When Mme. Monet awoke one morning near the end of their Venice sojourn, only the sound of pigeon-wings filled the air on the balcony where she stood listening. The birds of Venice had gone silent.

venice

red bluens green waters backgrounds alleyways where deep water wakens into sleep shape and form of softens it to absorb an eye-gaze that moves across absorbs so many reds piquant green history rides through them within yellow blue so many blues the earth as blue the water is blue stone yellow plaster dries the experiment of the eye names the name of being color-tone renaissance pigment here water through color flows flowing flow softens evenings rides through the plane of senses into the courtyard of proprioception the hand sees feeling the ear sees sound the curvature of time spells out the motion of everything is liquid as dawn yields to other light to follow dusk an explosion ringing reds to orange sky absorbs them together through swash of oar breaking word-soften color whisper surface home

my beautiful daughter

across the street a house is on fire its secret eye is burnt to a crisp its contents all destroyed I watch this from my bedroom window it is foretold I know it will happen someday to leave an empty lot a gap in space and time fills with weeds with tall devil grasses which I mow down with my imagination guarded by the four dogs of light and magic I had raised once myself from the depths of an everyone's anguish, quenched by drowning in deep seas where I had knelt to pray at the altar of water salt and whitewashed seashells I who am a fisher of gods emerging from schools of philosophy with my beautiful daughter at my side walking hand in hand into the moment of fire and water of sticks and wax of husbands and wives

2.
across the street from my small bedroom window I see that house on fire running in I grab the hand of my daughter to pull her out to safety she says to me oh my god papa the world is on fire the earth herself is burning up and you have saved only me

3.
by love's door I entered a fire discovering it was the only thing I had to live by it calmed my heart and made me the gentle man I am today

4.
robing myself in the fires only I walked down the boulevard just to see if it were the god it had become just as if it were the god my beautiful daughter saw when she looked in the mirrored horizon across the sea

5.
I refused to offer my beautiful daughter on the altar of fire it was her choice I said she left me but whether she's gone into the fire or whether she's wandered the earth lighting flames for every purpose wherever she went I'd imagine yet never know

&.

in my youth I knew a woman whom I thought would become my daughter she was older than me and wise we sat on a bench by the lake already she gave me a gift: the music of time I passed through her without having resolved the conflict between music and time when my daughter was born her mother, earth, holding her to her breast sang to her this lullaby the resolution of music and time is water is fire is breath is body is rhythm is mind

www.ingramcontent.com/pod-product-compliance
Lightning Source LLC
Chambersburg PA
CBHW041128110526
44592CB00020B/2724